The Marshall Cavendish Collection of

GREEN &

·WA1

C000259354

The Canals of the Midlands

MARSHALL CAVENDISH

Picture credits
A. Christiansen/ Frank Lane Picture Agency page 24. Robert Eames page 5, 8, 9, 12, 21. Mary Evans
Picture Library page 44. Paul Felix page 25, 28. Derek Forss page 17, 20, 33, 36. The Ironbridge Gorge
Museum page 29. Mansell Collection page 32. Derek Pratt page 13, 41. Jason Smalley page 37, 40.
Harry Smith page 16. All other pictures: Marshall Cavendish Picture Library

Art Editor: Joyce Mason
Designer: Richard Shiner
Editor: Irena Hoare
Picture Researcher: Vimu Patel
Production: Joanna Wilson

CONTENTS

GREEN & PLEASANT ——— WALKS ———

The walks in *GREEN & PLEASANT WALKS* will give you ideas for walks near your own neighbourhood, as well as in other areas of Britain.

All the walks are devised around a theme, and range in length from about 2 to 9 miles (3.25 to 14.5km). They vary in difficulty from very easy to mildly strenuous, and since each walk is circular, you will always end up back at your starting point.

Background information is given for many of the walks, relating legends, pointing out interesting buildings, giving details about famous people who have lived in the area. There are occasional 'Nature Facts' panels, which highlight some of the things you might see in the landscape as you walk.

THE LAW OF TRESPASS

If you find a right of way barred, the law says you may remove the obstruction, or take a short detour.

If the path is blocked by a field of crops, you may walk along the line of the path through the crops in single file. However, in England and Wales, if you stray from the path you are trespassing, and could be sued for damages.

If you do find that your path has been obstructed in some way, report the matter to the local authority, who will take the necessary action to clear the route.

It is illegal for farmers to place a bull on its own in a field crossed by a right of way (unless the bull is not a recognized dairy breed), but if you come across a bull on its own in a field, find another way round – and if you feel sufficiently aggrieved, report the farmer.

USING MAPS

Although this book of *GREEN & PLEASANT WALKS* gives you all the information you need to enjoy your walks, it is useful to have a larger scale map to give you detailed information about

---

THE COUNTRY CODE

- Enjoy the countryside, and respect the life and work of its inhabitants
- Always guard against any risk of fire
- Fasten all gates
- Keep your dogs under close control
- Keep to public footpaths across farmland
- Use gates and stiles to cross fences, hedges etc

- Leave livestock, crops and machinery alone
- Take your litter home with you
- Help to keep all water clean and unpolluted
- Protect wildlife, plants and trees
- Take special care on country roads
- Do not make any unnecessary noise

THE CANALS OF THE MIDLANDS

① Hilltop and Towpath ⑥ Forest of Arden

② Along the River Trent ⑦ Ironbridge Gorge

③ Along the Towpath ⑧ Shropshire's Lakes

④ Bosworth Field ⑨ Mill and Kilns

⑤ Midland Waterways ⑩ Cromford Canal

All walks featured in this book are plotted and numbered on the regional map below, and listed in the box (left).

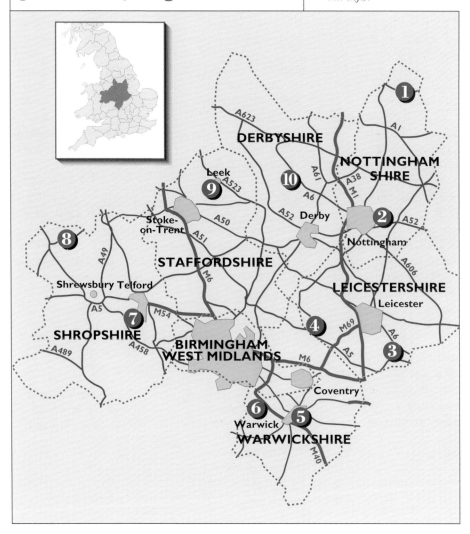

Canals of the Midlands

where you are. Britain is fortunate in having the best mapping agency in the world, the Ordnance Survey, which produces high-quality maps. The most useful of these for walkers are the 1:25,000 Pathfinder, Explorer and Outdoor Leisure maps. Use the grid references given in the fact files to help you find the starting point of each of the walks.

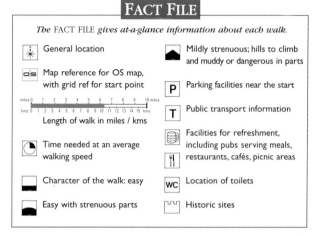

FACT FILE

The FACT FILE *gives at-a-glance information about each walk.*

✳	General location	▲	Mildly strenuous; hills to climb and muddy or dangerous in parts
OS	Map reference for OS map, with grid ref for start point	P	Parking facilities near the start
	Length of walk in miles / kms	T	Public transport information
◑	Time needed at an average walking speed	🍴	Facilities for refreshment, including pubs serving meals, restaurants, cafés, picnic areas
▬	Character of the walk: easy	WC	Location of toilets
◣	Easy with strenuous parts	🏰	Historic sites

miles 0 1 2 3 4 5 6 7 8 9 10 miles
kms 0 1 2 3 4 5 6 7 8 9 10 11 12 13 14 15 kms

GRID REFERENCES

All Ordnance Survey maps are over-printed with a framework of squares, called the National Grid. This is a reference system which, by breaking the country down into squares, lets you pinpoint an area and give it a unique number.

On OS Landranger, Pathfinder and Outdoor Leisure maps, a reference to an accuracy of 100m is possible. Grid squares on the maps cover an area of 1km x 1km on the ground.

GRID REFERENCES

Blenheim Palace, in Oxfordshire, has a grid reference of **SP 441 161**. This is constructed as follows:

SP: These letters identify the 100km grid square in which Blenheim Palace lies. The squares form the

basis of the National Grid. Information on the 100km square covering any given map is given in the map key.

441 161: This reference locates the position of Blenheim Palace to 100m in the 100km grid square.

44: This part of the reference is the number of the grid line which forms the western (left-hand) boundary of the 1km grid square in which Blenheim Palace appears. It is printed in the top and bottom margins of the relevant map (Pathfinder 1092 here).

16: This part of the reference is the number of the grid line which forms the southern boundary of the 1km grid square in which Blenheim Palace appears. The number is printed in the left and

right-hand margins of the relevant OS map (Pathfinder 1092 here).

Both numbers together (SP 4416) locate the bottom left-hand corner of the 1km grid square in which the Palace appears. The last figures in the reference **441 161** pinpoint the position in the square; dividing its western boundary lines into tenths and estimating on which imaginary tenths line the Palace lies.

Hilltop and Towpath

Along the Chesterfield Canal from an attractive hilltop village

Built over 200 years ago, the Chesterfield Canal winds gently across the countryside.

Gringley on the Hill has a remarkable position, spread along a ridge at the end of a range of low hills that stretches from Nottingham. The village is very attractive, with many fine houses on its steep hills.

The walk begins east of Beacon Hill **A**, a mound at the end of the ridge. Opinions vary as to whether it is a natural formation or not; some say it was built by the Romans, others that it contains a Viking burial.

From the top, the view stretches almost 30 miles (48km), with Lincoln Cathedral visible to the east on a clear day. The route heads across fields to the Chesterfield canal, past the pretty village of Wiseton **G** and on to Gringley Top Lock, before it returns to the village centre.

5

THE WALK

GRINGLEY ON THE HILL–CLAYWORTH–WISETON
The walk starts from a lay-by off the A631 at the eastern end of the village.

1 From the lay-by, walk down the High Street past Beacon Hill **A** and continue straight ahead through the village, passing the church **B** on your left, then bearing left by a cross **C**. Continue on the High Street as it bends right. Just past a white cottage on your left, take the signposted path to the main road (the A631) across a dry ditch. Cross with care to a signposted path opposite.

2 Go down a flight of wooden steps and cross the field diagonally right to a track. Turn right. Where the track ends, continue straight ahead across a field towards two trees. Step across a small ditch and go diagonally left to the far corner of the next field. Turn left along the headland, going slightly uphill. At the top of the rise, turn right along the headland. At the far end of the field, continue straight ahead along a grass track, which leads towards farm buildings.

3 Pass the buildings on your left, and bear left on the track. At the first hedge, turn right, and walk across an arable field to its far corner. Climb the stile and walk between a wire fence and a hedge. Pass through a gap in the hedge and follow a worn grass path to a signpost by a metalled road. Turn left towards the church **D**. Opposite the church, turn right down St Peter's Lane to pass Royston Manor Hotel **E** on your right. Cross the bridge over the canal **F**, and follow the towpath to the right for just over 1 mile (1.6km) to Wiseton **G**, passing under bridge No. 69.

4 Where the towpath joins a metalled road, turn right. Where the road bears away, rejoin the towpath; go under bridge No. 70. Follow the towpath for 1¼ miles (2km) to Drakeholes **H**.

5 At picnic site, turn onto main road; walk uphill across the tunnel. Cross main road with care. Take track opposite and follow it, left of farm buildings, as it becomes grassy. Follow it back to canal-side and continue under bridge No. 73A. Continue for 1¼ miles (2km) to Gringley Top Lock **J**.

6 Pass in front of lock-keeper's cottage, under bridge No. 74, left up steps. Turn left along road. After 350 yards (315m) take signposted path on left. Walk to far right corner of field. Climb stile, go diagonally right, heading to right of two barns. Climb two stiles ontoroad, and turn right. At the centre of Gringley, turn left to reach the start.

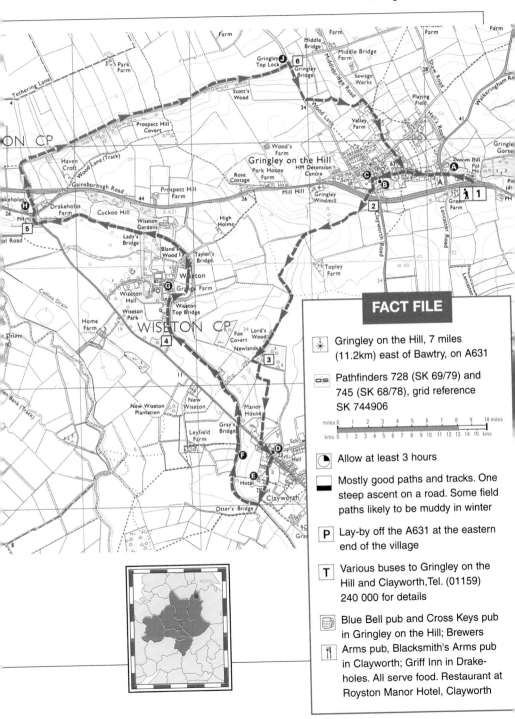

FACT FILE

Gringley on the Hill, 7 miles (11.2km) east of Bawtry, on A631

Pathfinders 728 (SK 69/79) and 745 (SK 68/78), grid reference SK 744906

miles 0 1 2 3 4 5 6 7 8 9 10 miles
kms 0 1 2 3 4 5 6 7 8 9 10 11 12 13 14 15 kms

Allow at least 3 hours

Mostly good paths and tracks. One steep ascent on a road. Some field paths likely to be muddy in winter

P Lay-by off the A631 at the eastern end of the village

T Various buses to Gringley on the Hill and Clayworth, Tel. (01159) 240 000 for details

Blue Bell pub and Cross Keys pub in Gringley on the Hill; Brewers Arms pub, Blacksmith's Arms pub in Clayworth; Griff Inn in Drakeholes. All serve food. Restaurant at Royston Manor Hotel, Clayworth

The Chesterfield Canal

The wide basin at Drakeholes gives boats plenty of room to manoeuvre.

This fine waterway was built at the end of the 18th century, when barges and narrowboats became the main means of transporting the raw materials and finished products of the burgeoning Industrial Revolution.

It was surveyed by the first great canal engineer, James Brindley, and completed five years after he died. The 46-mile (73.4-km) waterway, from Chesterfield to West Stockwith on the Trent, was opened on 4 June 1777.

Stone, corn, lead, bricks and general goods were carried, but the main cargo was coal. From West Stockwith, goods went on downriver with the tide or under sail.

The way the canal winds through the contours of the land, rather than cutting across them, is one clue to its early date. Extensive embankments and cuttings were too ambitious for the canal pioneers. The greatest feat of engineering on the canal was the 2,895-yard (2,730-m) Norwood Tunnel.

Like all canals, this one suffered in the 19th century from the competition of the railways. Trade declined, and it began to run at a loss. The Norwood Tunnel, whose roof collapsed several times, was closed in 1908.

After 1955, the waterway stopped being used commercially, though the towpath continued in use. In 1961, a group of enthusiasts teamed up to save the 26 navigable miles (41.6km) remaining. The Chesterfield Canal Society represents people with an interest in the canal; it is now working on the remaining 20 miles (32km), and hopes eventually to restore the canal to full working order.

Along The River Trent

A riverbank walk through a valley of fertile farmland

Wild flowers border the River Trent, which has been a trading route for centuries.

The walk is mostly on defined level footpaths along the banks of the River Trent. The river runs through a valley of mixed farmland, and is still often regarded as the dividing line between northern and southern England.

The walk takes you to the outskirts of Caythorpe, following a segment of the Trent Valley Way. A short road walk brings you to the old mill there, which is no longer in use, and to a path across the fields to the village of Gunthorpe.

River Traffic

The final stages follow a lane, with a brief road walk through the village back to the starting-point. The River Trent is busy here, popular with pleasure cruisers and

Continued on p. 12➤

THE WALK

GUNTHORPE–CAYTHORPE
The walk begins at the car park in
Gunthorpe, beside the River Trent.

1 From the car park, walk along the river banks in an easterly direction, away from Gunthorpe Bridge **Ⓐ**. At the end of the field keep to the bank, past the Toll House and Gunthorpe Marina on your left. Soon afterwards, pass the British Waterways Board offices and car park. Continue along Trent Valley Way **Ⓑ** to Gunthorpe Lock.

2 Go through the double white gates — a feature of this part of the River Trent **Ⓒ** — and walk along the bank for a little over 1 mile (1.6km), passing the two 17km and 18km markers. Opposite, the wooded slopes of the Trent Hills can be seen.

3 Shortly after passing the 18km marker, cross a footbridge and double gates. After 44 yards (40m) or so, bear diagonally left to a wooden stile in the corner of the field. Cross this and bear right, keeping to the edge of the field, until you reach the Hoveringham Road, gained by a stile beside a footpath sign.

4 Turn left and walk along Hoveringham Road for approximately 1/2 mile (800m) until you reach Caythorpe, with the Black Horse Inn on your right. Then turn left at Mill House; the path is signposted.

5 The path keeps to the right-hand side of the drive, passing the mill, with its wheel visible through a window. Keep to the right of the garage to gain a stile. Continue a short distance, with the field boundary on your right, to the next stile. When you have gone over the stile and then a footbridge, keep the field hedge on your left and you will reach another footbridge and, within about 100 yards (90m), yet another footbridge. Turn right here, keeping the field boundary on your right. After approximately 200 yards (180m), turn sharp left on a path that may be overgrown, and in another 200 yards (180m) you will gain a track beside a footpath sign. The footpath then becomes Peck Lane, and leads to the main road in Gunthorpe.

6 Turn left and walk along the main street, passing the Anchor Inn, Tom Brown's Bar and the Unicorn Hotel, until you arrive back at your starting-point.

Nature Facts

Fringed water lily. This flowers in July or August. Its floating leaves are purple underneath.

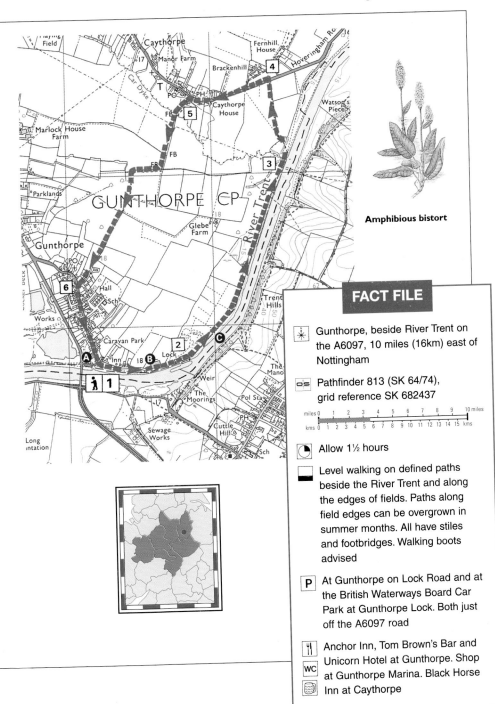

Amphibious bistort

FACT FILE

☀ Gunthorpe, beside River Trent on the A6097, 10 miles (16km) east of Nottingham

◻ Pathfinder 813 (SK 64/74), grid reference SK 682437

miles 0	1	2	3	4	5	6	7	8	9	10 miles
kms 0	1 2	3	4 5	6	7 8	9 10	11	12 13	14 15	kms

◕ Allow 1½ hours

▬ Level walking on defined paths beside the River Trent and along the edges of fields. Paths along field edges can be overgrown in summer months. All have stiles and footbridges. Walking boots advised

P At Gunthorpe on Lock Road and at the British Waterways Board Car Park at Gunthorpe Lock. Both just off the A6097 road

🍴 Anchor Inn, Tom Brown's Bar and Unicorn Hotel at Gunthorpe. Shop
WC at Gunthorpe Marina. Black Horse Inn at Caythorpe

narrowboats, which use Gunthorpe Lock to avoid boating through the weir.

The walk begins beside the River Trent, with views to the wooded slopes of the Trent Hills on the eastern side of the river. The first half of the walk is along the banks of the navigable river, passing Gunthorpe Lock and having views of the impressive Gunthorpe Weir.

A popular water-ski club operates near Gunthorpe Bridge, and there are lots of birds to watch out for, including the grey heron. After visiting the old mill at Caythorpe, which still has its water-wheel, you return over the fields.

The road bridge at Gunthorpe ❹ is the only one over the river between the towns of Newark and Nottingham, a distance of 24 miles (39km). Today's bridge was built in 1927. Before 1875, when the first bridge at this location was built, a ferry operated here, crossing the river to East Bridgford.

The River Trent runs through a valley of mixed farmland.

Trent Valley Way

The early section of the walk follows the Trent Valley Way ❸. This is a long-distance footpath that runs alongside the River Trent from the northern boundary of Nottinghamshire to Nottingham. The River Trent ❻ is one of the major rivers of the Midlands, navigable from here to the Humber, a distance of about 11 miles (16.6km). Including the lock at Gunthorpe, the river has 12 locks. Two Bronze Age canoes were found in the river bed near Nottingham, suggesting it was used as a trading route as early as 1000 BC.

History of the River

The Romans built the Foss Dyke in AD 120, linking the River Trent to the River Witham at Lincoln. The Vikings ventured up here on their raids. Some of the oldest bridges in England span the Trent; one of them, in Nottingham, stood for 714 years.

An Act of Parliament was passed in 1699, to make the river navigable, but it was not until an Act of 1783 that towpaths were built, and the Trent Navigation Company was formed. Locks and weirs were built and sections were deepened.

During the 19th century, the river was a major artery in the waterways of the Midlands. Further work was completed in 1926 which dramatically increased traffic. However competition from the railways and, later, the roads eventually greatly reduced its commercial use.

Along the Towpath

A canalside walk through the quiet countryside of Leicestershire

There is always plenty to watch at Foxton flight, with its two sets of five locks.

The great attraction of this canal walk is the combination of the quiet undulating countryside of south Leicestershire and the general activity of canal boats moving through the locks. Cut off from road traffic, there is complete freedom to walk along the towpaths and enjoy the special attractions that canals have to offer. Wildlife abounds around the canals, which provide a haven for birds such as mallards and moorhens – even the occasional kingfisher – and for small mammals such as the elusive water vole.

A Flight of Locks

Originally canals were built for carrying freight. Today they are mostly plied by pleasure craft carrying families on holiday.

Continued on p. 16➤

13

THE WALK

FOXTON LOCKS–FOXTON
The walk begins at the car park and picnic site just beyond Foxton village.

1 From the car park, turn left along the pedestrian way until you reach the canal. Pass under the road bridge, then over the canal by the new footbridge on to the towpath. The canal will now be on your right. Walk down the towpath to reach the Keeper's Cottage and the top lock in the flight ❶. Cross the little footbridges to explore the inclined plane, the reconstructed engine house and the small museum ❷.

2 At the bottom lock, pass under the bridge and continue to the canal junction with the Market Harborough branch. Walk along the towpath, cross over the next bridge, then walk down the towpath with the canal now on your left side. Follow the path north as far as Debdale Wharf (Bridge No. 65). Keep on the towpath, ignoring the overgrown path on the right.

3 Retrace your steps the way you came. When you reach the point where the canal bends right, you have a choice of routes. You can return the way you came, back to the locks, or follow a bridleway across the fields to Foxton village. This route can be muddy, slippery and rutted in bad weather. If you want to take it, follow instructions 4 to 7 below.

4 At the bend in the canal, turn left up a little path which ascends steeply up the embankment to join with the bridleway at the top. Follow the bridleway round the left-hand side of the field, then bear right along the far edge of the same field, keeping the hedge on your left, to reach the marker post where the hedge ends.

5 From the marker post walk directly across the field towards a telegraph pole (with red brick buildings behind it) and the large metal gates by the lane. If the field has been ploughed or cropped, follow the horse tracks down to the small stream, turn left then follow the bank of the stream to reach the gates.

6 On reaching the lane, turn right and walk along the lane to join the Main Streeet in Foxton village ❷ by the canal bridge. Turn right over the bridge and go up the road past the church.

7 Continue along the road back to the car park at the starting point.

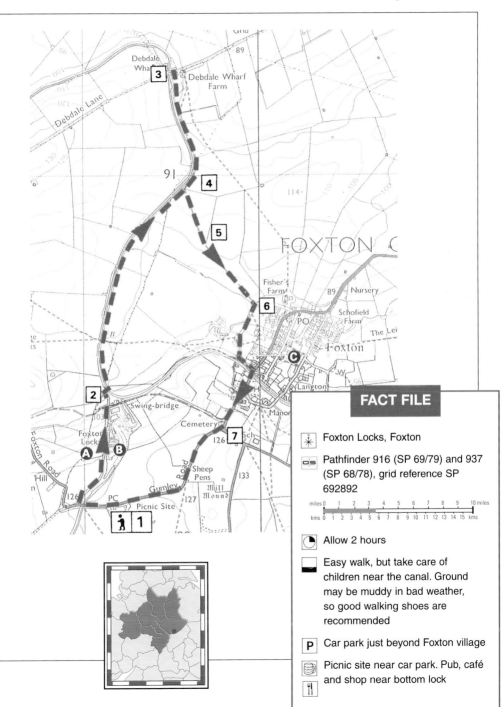

FACT FILE

Foxton Locks, Foxton

Pathfinder 916 (SP 69/79) and 937 (SP 68/78), grid reference SP 692892

miles 0 1 2 3 4 5 6 7 8 9 10 miles
kms 0 1 2 3 4 5 6 7 8 9 10 11 12 13 14 15 kms

Allow 2 hours

Easy walk, but take care of children near the canal. Ground may be muddy in bad weather, so good walking shoes are recommended

P Car park just beyond Foxton village

Picnic site near car park. Pub, café and shop near bottom lock

Locks are an essential feature of canals, constructed to overcome the differences between water levels. Single locks are used where the change in level is slight, but a flight of locks is needed at Foxton where the gradient is steep.

This walk includes the Foxton flight of ten narrow locks 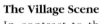 and the remains of Foxton Inclined Plane ❸, built to take boats up and down the steep hillside.

The flight is one of the most remarkable features of Britain's canals. It was built between 1806 and 1814, forming part of the Grand Union Canal's link across the uplands of Northamptonshire to the Grand Junction Canal at Long Buckby. The flight was seen as a considerable feat of engineering, succeeding in raising or lowering vessels 75 feet (23m). However, passage through the locks was slow – it took vessels over 70 minutes – and the locks became a bottleneck. As a result the inclined plane was designed to bypass the locks.

The striking yellow flag iris grows on the banks of canals and ponds.

The Inclined Plane

At the turn of the century rails were laid in the side of the hill to take two baths or wheeled boxes full of water, each large enough to carry two narrow boats. They were counter-balanced so that the ascending bath was lifted by the weight of its descending partner. The system took only 12 minutes, but it was expensive to run and by about 1910, as canal traffic declined, the incline went out of use and was later dismantled. Today restorers are planning to rebuild the plane, and there is a museum and a reconstructed engine house for visitors to look at.

This lovely walk continues along the towpath towards Debdale Wharf. When the wharf opened for trading in 1797, Derbyshire coal, which was an important fuel, was sold at 11d (about 5p) per hundredweight.

The Village Scene

In contrast to the busy canal scene, a walk across the fields ends in the peaceful countryside village of Foxton. Nestling on either side of the Market Harborough arm of the Grand Union Canal, this area was once a favourite hunting ground of John of Gaunt, the brother of the Black Prince, and father of Henry IV.

John of Gaunt was once the Lord of the Manor at Foxton ❸, and the manor house can still be seen near St Andrew's church. The building dates mainly from the 13th and 14th centuries, although there are earlier features, such as a fine Norman font.

Bosworth Field

Walking to the site of the battle
that ended the Wars of the Roses

Though a peaceful place today, Bosworth field was once the scene of fierce combat.

The Battle of Bosworth Field on 22 August 1485 was one of the great turning points in English history. The death of King Richard III, and the defeat of his forces by those of Henry Tudor, ended the long, unstable period of the Wars of the Roses – a struggle for the throne of England fought between the royal families of Lancaster and York. This was achieved in an encounter that lasted only an hour, and took the form of brutal and clumsy hand-to-hand combat.

A Pastoral Coronation

The battle was the last occasion on which a King of England died fighting in battle. Henry was crowned Henry VII — it is said that the crown was found behind a bush

Continued on p. 20 ➤

17

THE WALK

BOSWORTH FIELD – SUTTON CHENEY
The walk begins at the Cheney Lane car park.

1 With your back to the entrance of the car park, take the clearly waymarked path from the right-hand corner. Keep to the right of the next four fields, before arriving at the Battlefield Visitor Centre **Ⓐ**.

2 Take the way-marked path leading from the Centre to a stile on the other side of Ambion Wood.

3 Cross over the stile, and follow the path along the canal **Ⓑ** to a car park and bridge at Sutton Wharf.

4 Turn left along Wharf Lane to Sutton Cheney **Ⓒ**.

5 Take the first left, at Ambion Lane, to return to the car park and the start of the walk.

Nature Facts

Swallow. This familiar summer visitor is often found near water. It returns each year to the same mud and straw nest.

Little grebe (adult). Also called a dabchick, this bird is the smallest of the grebe family. Its nest is made of floating weeds.

Little grebe (juvenile). The baby grebe soon learns to bob and dive for the small fish that make up its diet.

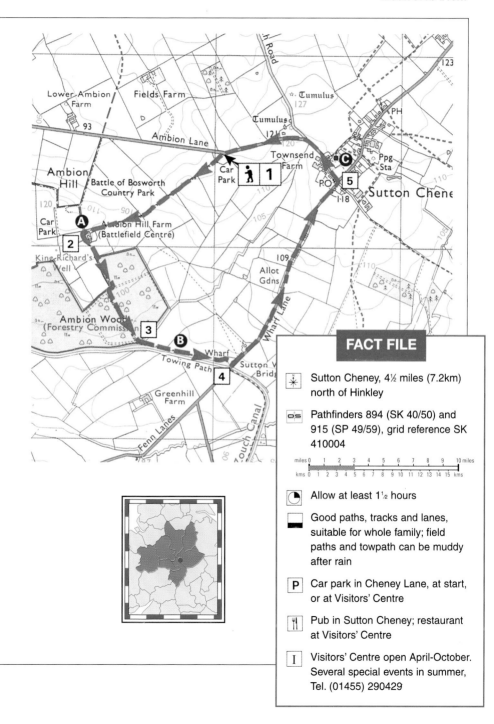

FACT FILE

Sutton Cheney, 4½ miles (7.2km) north of Hinkley

Pathfinders 894 (SK 40/50) and 915 (SP 49/59), grid reference SK 410004

miles 0 1 2 3 4 5 6 7 8 9 10 miles
kms 0 1 2 3 4 5 6 7 8 9 10 11 12 13 14 15 kms

Allow at least 1½ hours

Good paths, tracks and lanes, suitable for whole family; field paths and towpath can be muddy after rain

P Car park in Cheney Lane, at start, or at Visitors' Centre

Pub in Sutton Cheney; restaurant at Visitors' Centre

I Visitors' Centre open April-October. Several special events in summer, Tel. (01455) 290429

while Richard's men were still being slaughtered, and was placed on Henry's head with the battle still raging. Henry established the Tudor dynasty, which brought prosperity and stability at home, as well as power and great conquests abroad. The dynasty finally ended in 1601, when Queen Elizabeth I died without producing an heir, and the throne passed to the Stuarts of Scotland.

This walk explores the site of the historic battle, now pleasant farmland, and the country surrounding it. It begins at the car park for the Visitors' Centre **A**, near the hamlet of Sutton Cheney. Most of the actual fighting took place on Ambion Hill, close to here, but the battle was named after the small town of Market Bosworth, which lies on the sky-line to the north. The excellent displays in the Visitors'

The old almshouses in Sutton Cheney have been converted into tea-rooms.

Centre are augmented by events throughout the summer, while the well laid-out and very informative Battlefield Trail gives an account of the battle, and the events that led up to it.

Ashby Canal

From the Visitor Centre you walk through the conifers of Ambion Wood to the Ashby

Canal **B**, which was built between 1794 and 1804 to transport coal from the coalfields in the north-west of the country to Hinckley and Leicester. It was never a very successful venture, and was superseded in the 1830s by the Leicester to Swannington Railway, one of the earliest lines to be built in Britain.

Where the canal is crossed by a lane at Sutton Wharf, you turn up the quiet road to Sutton Cheney **C**. The ill-fated Richard III marched through here from Leicester with his troops, before camping out on Ambion Hill, the night before the great battle.

The quaint 14th-century church was already standing then, and tradition has it that Richard attended his last Mass here on the morning before the battle. To the east of the church is an attractive row of almshouses, which were founded in 1612. They are now open to the public, and visitors can find tea, food and lodgings here.

Just outside the village, as you walk down another lane back to the car park, you pass an early Bronze Age burial mound. Richard III is said to have addressed his forces at this ancient site on the eve of the battle.

Midland Waterways

From a peaceful hillside village
through quiet farmlands

Napton Locks is where the Oxford Canal drops to join the Grand Union Canal.

The village of Napton, where the walk begins, is very much 'on the hill', standing high above the surrounding countryside. From the village there is a short stroll across fields to a lane that leads down to the valley. Part-way down there is a splendid view of the locks **A** on the Oxford Canal and of the tower windmill — a prominent landmark at the

top of the hill. Further down are flooded clay pits, producing clay that is used for brick-making. By the canal are the stables, reminders that the working boats on the canal were once all pulled by horses.

Brindley's Canal

The next section of the walk follows the towpath. The building of the canal started

Continued on p. 24➤

21

THE WALK

NAPTON ON THE HILL–UPPER SHUCKBURGH–LOWER SHUCKBURGH
The walk starts at the triangular green in the
centre of Napton on the Hill.

1 With your back to the Crown Inn, take the footpath to the left, past the thatched cottage. Take the path along the boundary of the cottage (it may be overgrown), cross the stile and head over the field to the road; turn right.

2 At the road junction turn left past the view of Napton locks **A** to the canal.

3 Cross the bridge over the canal, turn right to join the towpath, then left onto the towpath, away from the bridge.

4 Leave the towpath by turning left just before the bridge at Napton marina. Cross the road to the stile, and take the footpath diagonally across to the opposite corner.

5 Take the path up to Napton Reservoirs **B** bank, turn left and follow the path round to the right across the bridge. At the canal, turn left. Cross the canal at the lock.

6 Go through the gap in the hedge by the bottom lock gates, through the iron gate, and left to follow the line of the hedge to the gate. Beyond the gate turn right along the edge of the field and past the small wood.

7 Where the track swings left, carry straight on up the rise, and down the bank to join the towpath. Turn left and leave the towpath to cross the canal on the footbridge. Follow the fence round to the gate at right of church.

8 Cross the main road, turn left. Cross the stile beside the cottage, take the footpath across the fields towards the farm. The path across the fields is waymarked by yellow arrows towards the hill crowned by woods.

9 Where the path divides near top of hill, follow along edge of woodland, over top of Beacon Hill **C**.

10 At edge of woods, follow track to the right; head down hill towards barns. The path has been routed to cut across corner of the field, then follows the edge of the field to protect crops.

11 At the road, turn left, then right on the far side of the fence. Watch out for a gap in the fence where the path cuts right across the field and to a stile, then continues over stiles to the road.

12 Turn right. At the junction turn left, signposted to Napton.

13 At next junction, right up lane.

14 At main road, turn left, return to start.

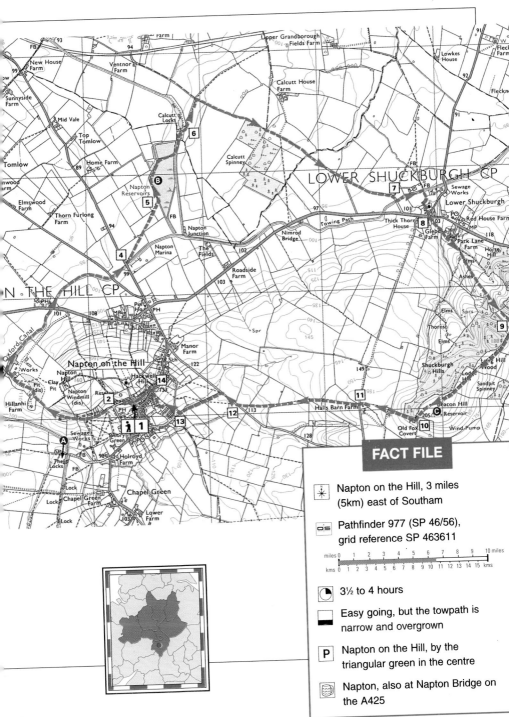

FACT FILE

Napton on the Hill, 3 miles
(5km) east of Southam

Pathfinder 977 (SP 46/56),
grid reference SP 463611

miles 0 1 2 3 4 5 6 7 8 9 10 miles
kms 0 1 2 3 4 5 6 7 8 9 10 11 12 13 14 15 kms

3½ to 4 hours

Easy going, but the towpath is
narrow and overgrown

P Napton on the Hill, by the
triangular green in the centre

Napton, also at Napton Bridge on
the A425

in 1769, and James Brindley, the chief engineer, followed his usual practice of running it along the natural contours of the land, so that it snakes its way around the hill. The towpath is narrow and often overgrown in summer, so walkers have to move in single file.

The canal banks are a delight for lovers of wild flowers: on one side you have a range of hedgerow plants; on the other the reeds and water plants.

There are still reminders of the old life of the canal. The first road bridge has been widened to allow for the needs of modern traffic, but you can still see how the original bridge was built on the skew, involving a complex pattern of bricklaying.

Beyond the bridge there is a widened section of the canal, known as a winding hole. These sections were necessary, to allow the 70-foot (21m)- long old working narrowboats to be turned around.

Mallards such as this one thrive on the Napton reservoirs.

Wide Locks

The walk now leaves the canal and takes you across fields to Napton Reservoirs ❸. These were built to supply water for the canal, and are now very popular with water birds of all kinds. Beyond is another canal, the Grand Union, which was built later than the Oxford. It has wide locks able to take two narrowboats, side by side. You cross fields and walk through woods, before rejoining the Oxford Canal by a dismantled bridge.

Leaving the canal, the walk goes past the curious little gothic church of Lower Shuckburgh. The interior is even more remarkable than the exterior, with bright red brick pillars and arches.

The path now leads steadily up the grassy hill towards a knoll crowned with trees. It runs close to a large private wood on one side, where there is an attractive lake. Shuckburgh Park can be seen to the left, with its chapel and home farm.

The route runs along the ridge of the hills; from the summit ❸ there are fine views of the countryside. Napton Hill can be seen, as can the tall telecommunications tower and the complex of masts that marks the radio station at Daventry. Closer by there is a medieval farming landscape, the old pattern of ridge and furrow visible under the grass.

The path leads back down to the valley, where it skirts round, or cuts through, fields as it takes you back to Napton.

The Forest of Arden

Mellow countryside and a towpath walk in the heart of England

Timber-framed cottages in Henley-in-Arden make a picturesque start to the walk.

The small town of Henley-in-Arden **Ⓐ** is the starting point for this walk. It is a pretty town whose High Street is a living museum of English vernacular architecture. Medieval cottages rub eaves with well-restored yeoman's houses and ancient coaching inns.

The walk starts by the 15th-century church of St John, which juts resolutely into the main street, and continues down a lane to the Norman Beaudesert church **Ⓑ**. This was the original parish church, but was replaced by St John's because it tended to get flooded in wintertime.

De Montfort Castle

A little further on is a hill **Ⓒ** that was the site of an 11th-century castle, the seat of

Continued on p. 28➤

THE WALK

HENLEY-IN-ARDEN–PRESTON BAGOT
The walk begins in Henley High Street **Ⓐ**.

1 Start by walking along Beaudesert Lane, beside St John's Church. Cross the River Alne and walk past the Church of St Nicholas **Ⓑ**. As the lane twists sharp right, keep ahead to pass through the kissing gate.

2 Take the direction indicated by the waymark arrow, and go over the hill **Ⓒ** on which the de Montfort castle was situated. Keep along the clear path to climb a ridge, where there are two step stiles. Climb the right-hand one of these to enter a pasture.

3 Walk to the right of the electricity line, to a stile into a lane. Turn left and follow the lane to Kate's Cottage. Go through the metal gate on the right, keeping to the hedge on the left. Before the end of the field, go through a green metal gate.

4 Cross the field, aiming to the right of the farmstead. Go over a waymarked stile, then over another stile by a barn. Cross the lane to continue on the path opposite. Walk up the hill and go past Preston Bagot church **Ⓓ** to a lane. Cross over a marked fence stile to a path.

5 Descend through a pasture and walk to the end of the next field. Cross the bridge and go past the tea rooms, then go over a lane to the canalside. Cross the water and turn right along the towpath. Preston Bagot Manor House **Ⓔ** is on your right just before you go under the B4095.

6 Continue along the canal for approximately 1¼ miles (2km). Turn right along a tarmac farm drive, go over a bridge and pass the field with the moated house outline. Turn right on the road alongside the osier beds **Ⓕ**.

7 Climb a stile into the meadow on the left. Walk diagonally across the field to the far side, and go over another stile by the river. Turn right, and keep near to the river until you reach Blackford Mill **Ⓖ**. Turn left along the drive, then immediately right over the weir. Follow the path to the playing field. Bear slightly right to the main road, where you turn right to return to Henley and the starting point.

Nature Facts

Ruffe. This common fish feeds by day on the muddy bottoms of canals and slow rivers.

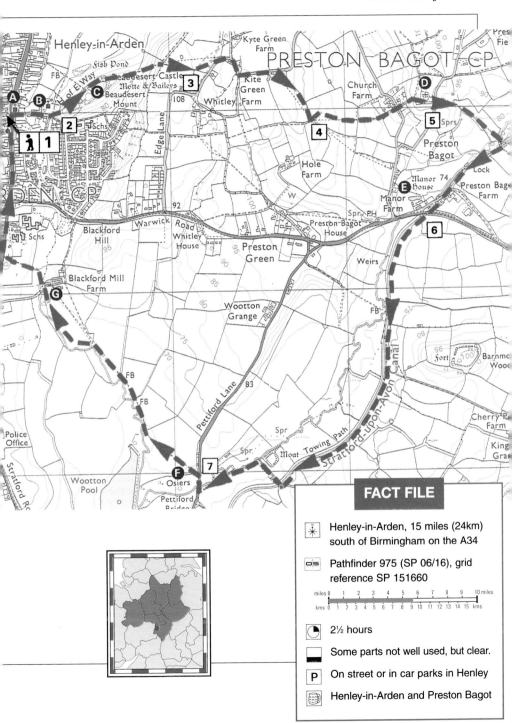

FACT FILE

Henley-in-Arden, 15 miles (24km) south of Birmingham on the A34

OS Pathfinder 975 (SP 06/16), grid reference SP 151660

miles 0 1 2 3 4 5 6 7 8 9 10 miles
kms 0 1 2 3 4 5 6 7 8 9 10 11 12 13 14 15 kms

2½ hours

Some parts not well used, but clear.

P On street or in car parks in Henley

Henley-in-Arden and Preston Bagot

the de Montfort family. The fortunes of the castle declined after the lord of the manor, Peter, was slain with his kinsman, Simon de Montfort, at the Battle of Evesham in 1265. Little is left of the castle today.

Rabbits burrow in the soft soil of the hill, which gives views over the flat lands that once formed the vast Forest of Arden. Small pockets of that ancient woodland still remain.

The walk continues through farmland to the scattered hamlet of Preston Bagot, with its fine hilltop church **D**. It drops down to the valley of a fast-flowing brook, and then follows the towpath of the Stratford-upon-Avon Canal.

Restored Canal

The canal was built between 1793 and 1816 to join the Grand Union Canal with the Worcester and Birmingham Canal. The longboats carried mostly coal on the southbound journey and returned laden with wheat and lime.

Trade dropped off at the end of the 19th century, and the waterway was derelict for many years. It came into the hands of the National Trust, and after restoration by enthusiastic bands of volunteers, it was reopened to traffic in 1964. It is now busy

The steeply pitched roof of Blackford Mill suggests it was once thatched.

a lot of the time, especially with pleasure boats in the summer.

Among the features to look out for on the way are bridges with slits down the middle so that the towing horses did not have to be unhitched, and lock-keepers' cottages with barrel roofs, perhaps adapted from templates for bridges.

Not long after joining the towpath, you will see a restored, timber-framed house, Preston Bagot Manor House **E**, on the other side of the water. After leaving the waterway, the route crosses pasture and meadowland and then briefly joins a road past some osier beds **F**, where willow trees were regularly coppiced to provide the raw material for wicker basketmakers.

The final part of the walk follows the course of the River Alne. Tench (a kind of fish) thrive in the pools of this slow-moving stream, which is also home to ducks and swans and increasingly large flocks of Canada geese. The latter are becoming a problem to the farmers of the neighbourhood.

From Blackford Mill Farm **G**, where flour was ground from local crops for hundreds of years, it is a short walk back along the road to Henley.

Ironbridge Gorge

An area of Britain's industrial heritage in spectacular scenery

The elegant structure of the world's oldest cast-iron bridge spans the Severn.

Ironbridge Gorge has been designated a world heritage site for the wealth of attractions and sights that it has to offer. It is known as the birthplace of the industrial revolution, which occurred due to the fortuitous combination of coal, iron, transport and water power.

The iron industry of the area was closely associated with the family of Abraham Darby and the firm he founded, the Coalbrookdale Company. The name of the valley is derived from the world's first iron bridge. It spans the River Severn.

Ironbridge itself is perched on limestone cliffs in the middle of magnificent Shropshire countryside. The area is unique, as it has remained almost totally undeveloped for over a hundred years.

29

THE WALK

IRONBRIDGE GORGE
The walk begins at the exit from the Visitor Centre's
car park, Museum of the River, Ironbridge.

1 Left on road, right up Station Road. Continue over rise; right fork down hill, right under bridge. Pass museum **Ⓐ**, on left; up to main road.

2 Cross to Church Rd and go up to church **Ⓑ**; left over stile to wood, immediately left, then right up steps; after 40 steps, right through wood. Left on road, past pub.

3 Cross to public path; track veers left, but go forward by hedge on right, through barrier, down road. Left at junction for short way, right to Belle Vue Rd. Follow as it narrows, to junction.

4 For short walk, sharp right to St Luke's Rd. Left at church **Ⓒ** for few yards, right down steps, through tunnel to Ironbridge. Right back to start.

5 Or continue forward, ignoring left turn to

At junction, right to Belmont Rd. Keep right and downhill; cross busy road carefully. Down path opposite, right of building with tower. Left of pub, right at junction to pass car park. Soon fork right; follow road to left; ignore track from left, but then bear left on track towards cottage.

6 Right of cottage, up bank (path faint/overgrown), cross clearing; follow power lines. At end, half-left into wood and ascend steps, fork right up more steps to clearing. To right of notice **Ⓓ**; cross. Pass pool on left, straight on at junction. Path winds through wood, at times faint, steps confirm route. Left on path coming from right, follow edge of wood, swing sharp left, track leads to road. Go up hill, half-right

Continued on p. 32 ➡

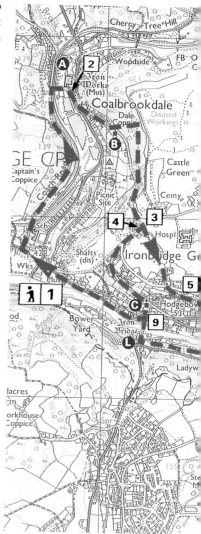

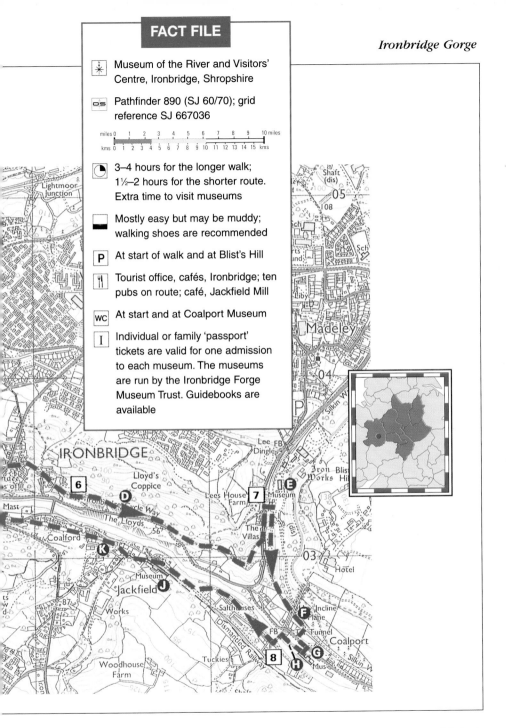

FACT FILE

※	Museum of the River and Visitors' Centre, Ironbridge, Shropshire
☷	Pathfinder 890 (SJ 60/70); grid reference SJ 667036

miles 0 1 2 3 4 5 6 7 8 9 10 miles
kms 0 1 2 3 4 5 6 7 8 9 10 11 12 13 14 15 kms

◗	3–4 hours for the longer walk; 1½–2 hours for the shorter route. Extra time to visit museums
▬	Mostly easy but may be muddy; walking shoes are recommended
P	At start of walk and at Blist's Hill
¶↾	Tourist office, cafés, Ironbridge; ten pubs on route; café, Jackfield Mill
WC	At start and at Coalport Museum
I	Individual or family 'passport' tickets are valid for one admission to each museum. The museums are run by the Ironbridge Forge Museum Trust. Guidebooks are available

Origins of the Iron Industry

Coalbrookdale by Night *(1801), by Philippe Jacques de Loutherbourg.*
This is a romanticized depiction of early blast furnaces.

Iron ore was first produced on a commercial basis in 1709, due to the innovations of Abraham Darby, a Quaker ironmaster. He used coke, instead of the traditional charcoal, to smelt the ore, making it possible for iron to be mass-produced. This gave rise to a new industry in the area.

across parking area to 'Trades' entrance, but before this, half-left, then left down steps.

7 Right for museum **E**, left into tunnel. Follow Silkin Trail, under bridge **F**, right down steps by markers. Cross road, left on path, right at entrance of works **G**. Before bridge **H**, right down steps, left over other bridge. Follow canal to bridge over Severn, cross.

8 Right on road/path. Pass mill, then forwards, past houses, to river. Follow up hill; when road bends left, go forward, towards river, up to church. Continue to museum **J**, turn right; at junction, right. Where road swings right at crossing, follow rail line **K** to car park. Exit far right, to bridge.

9 Cross bridge **L**. Turn left along the river to return to start of walk.

Shropshire's Lake District

Through farmland, alongside a canal and beside lakes rich in birdlife

The peaceful Cole Mere has a country park on its eastern shore.

Although the area of this walk is usually known as the Shropshire Lake District, this is a misnomer. These expanses of water are meres — not lakes. Lakes have streams or rivers flowing in and out of them, while meres do not. However, the word 'mere' is of Anglo Saxon origin and means 'lake'. Here they are referred to either as lakes or meres.

The walk explores three meres, and the abundant wildlife on their shores.

The group of meres at Ellesmere is the largest in the country and 'the Mere', is the greatest of these. It used to be much larger, surrounding the old town on three sides as a natural fortification. In 1805, however, the level was lowered artificially to allow the town to expand.

33

THE WALK

ELLESMERE–WELSHAMPTON–COLE MERE–ELLESMERE

The walk begins at the car park next to the Mere **A**.

1 Follow lakeside path to Ellesmere. Near church enter Cremorne Gardens **B**. Follow path around Mere, past island **C**, 'Neddy Jebb's Island'. At other side of lake, path crosses three stiles. Third marks end of path. After crossing this, turn left and follow fence and hedge on left. (This may be overgrown.) Cross stile, and continue with hedge on left to another fence. Path shown on OS map now re-routed. Right along this wire fence to corner of a small field, left to Crimps Farm. Top strand of wire is electrified. Go through galvanized gate into lane.

2 Right along lane, until it ends at a gate. This path also re-routed, so left round the field and up to derelict house by top corner. Continue along marked path between fence and woods. From next gate follow marked path, but as it bears right, branch off left, at a tangent, to stile in fence. Cross next field; head towards right of a small wood, to gate in top corner of field. Cross stile, with fence to right, pass to left of pond. Continue and pass small mere (fenced) also on the right. Keep fence on right, go ahead to gate into a lane.

3 Follow lane to farm and A495. (Take care on busy road.) Right along road. Just past the second cottage on left, left turn into lane marked 'Unsuitable for Motors'. Follow this, crossing a minor road, until canal.

4 Cross canal bridge, follow lane past a house until you reach gate to turn left to 'Boathouse Wood'. Path continues around edge of Cole Mere past boathouse and club to grassland and exposed shoreline **D**, with picnic area. Cross this to a gate to Yell Wood. (There is no access to water's edge.)

5 Path goes through wood to join canal towpath. Follow this left to Yell Bridge **E**. It then goes back to wood and continues to canalside buildings by Bridge 55, which you crossed earlier. Go through gate to road and back over bridge to towpath going to the left down a steep bank.

6 Follow path, canal on left, to Blake Mere. Here path goes along narrow spit of land between mere and canal. At far end of mere follow path through tunnel **F**. At other end, right immediately to climb to road. Exit from canal towpath leads to A495 (take care crossing to path on far side – drivers are not aware of this exit). Follow the road left, which will return you to the starting point of the walk.

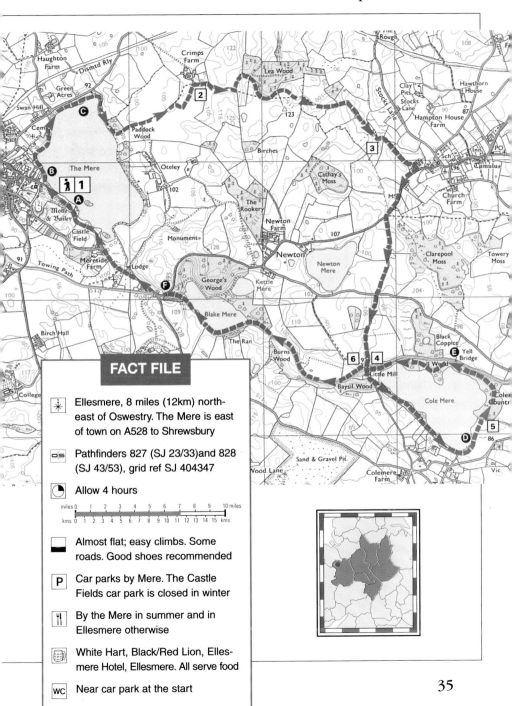

FACT FILE

※ Ellesmere, 8 miles (12km) north-east of Oswestry. The Mere is east of town on A528 to Shrewsbury

▱ Pathfinders 827 (SJ 23/33)and 828 (SJ 43/53), grid ref SJ 404347

◕ Allow 4 hours

miles 0 1 2 3 4 5 6 7 8 9 10 miles
kms 0 1 2 3 4 5 6 7 8 9 10 11 12 13 14 15 kms

▬ Almost flat; easy climbs. Some roads. Good shoes recommended

P Car parks by Mere. The Castle Fields car park is closed in winter

🍴 By the Mere in summer and in Ellesmere otherwise

🍺 White Hart, Black/Red Lion, Ellesmere Hotel, Ellesmere. All serve food

WC Near car park at the start

35

The Making of the Meres

With an area of 116 acres (50 ha), the Mere is the largest of the waters at Ellesmere. Herons nest in the trees.

As the last Ice Age was coming to an end — about 12,000 years ago — glaciers from Scotland, the Lake District and North Wales were converging upon the Shropshire and Cheshire plain, and melting.

The rocks, sand and, importantly, the boulder clay that had been scoured from other areas was deposited on the central plain in very large quantities.

This process possibly continued for · centuries, and the moraines (debris) left behind are extensive.

Huge ice blocks had been pressed down into the clay, so when the ice melted the surface of the plain was undulating and pitted.

Some of these pits are steep-sided and are known as kettle holes. They became filled with water and, even today, thousands of these 'puddles' are spread over the area.

Most have no stream or river flowing in or out, yet they remain full of water, because of the water table lying only a few feet below the ground. Water, carrying many nutrients with it, seeps up through the clay, which is why the meres have a great abundance of plant, fish and other wildlife living in or near them.

The formation and natural maintenance of lakes in this way is unique in the British Isles, and is rare generally, throughout the world.

Mill and Kilns

Follow a little-known river valley
to a woodland nature reserve

An old limekiln beside Caldon Canal is a reminder of the valley's industrial past.

The walk passes through a corner of Staffordshire that gloriously lays the lie that the county has been ruined by heavy industry.

The River Churnet winds through a wooded gorge. The scenery is not disturbed by roads. There was once industry here, but it was served by canal, river and rail, leaving the countryside peaceful.

Cheddleton village **A** sits astride the ancient trade route betwen Buxton and Stafford. The heart of the village lies up a sunken lane, at the start of the walk.

Terraces of tiny cottages and larger yeomen's houses huddle opposite a 12th-century church of mellow sandstone. The village's former industrial centre lies below, at the foot of a steep bluff.

THE WALK

CHEDDLETON–CONSALL

The walk starts by the parish church in Cheddleton **A**.

1 Walk down Hollow Lane. Left, then left again at sign to Mill **B**.

2 Leave Mill, left down path, with canal **C** on right. At bridge make detour, left, to station **D**. Continue on path. At lock **E**, cross canal, follow river past lime-kilns **F** to Consallforge **G**.

3 Rejoin path below pub. Pass under railway, follow canal to high overbridge. Cross canal . Left over stile, cross bridge. Left, then right over small bridge. Follow marks up steps, through wood **H**, out of it, down to wood.

4 Quite soon, cross bridge, climb steps. Left at top, leave marked route. At head of narrowing valley, cross bridge. Path leaves woods, crosses car park to road. Right.

5 Where road bends left, go right on a signed path; cross stiles. Go half-left to the offset, dog-leg corner of field. Cross stile, go diagonally across large field. Where hedge meets woodland, cross stile to woods on far side. Descend to stream.

6 Ford stream at sharp bend. Just beyond are a capped shaft and a sign for wood **J**. Follow yellow arrows up to and across a track. Path faint. If you lose sight of marks, keep right until you reach wider track by pond filled with tree stumps. Left, then bear right on marked path through woods, keep right if in doubt.

7 Stile out of woods. Slightly left to stile in far corner. Follow hedge to your right, then a field-side track to farm. Through yard to road. Right, then left after short way on path signed 'Folley Lane'. Cross stile ahead and go up long field to farm. Pass between house and barn. Cross track, to Spout House Farm.

8 Walk left of barn. Through enclosed farmyard, along drive. At crossing drive, through left-hand gate, follow line of hedge on right to stile. Climb it, turn right. Stiles; on to Woodlands Hall.

9 On through yard to field. Stay by hedge on left. Cross stile, down field, hedge to left. Two more stiles ahead, follow track down through ford, up between farm and works.Road bends right, through middle gate ahead, follow hedge. Through gate, follow path to inn at Basford Bridge.

10 Walk in front of terrace opposite pub, along path beyond. Second right fork to canal, below garden. Remain with path, leave canal, cross fields to Cheddleton.

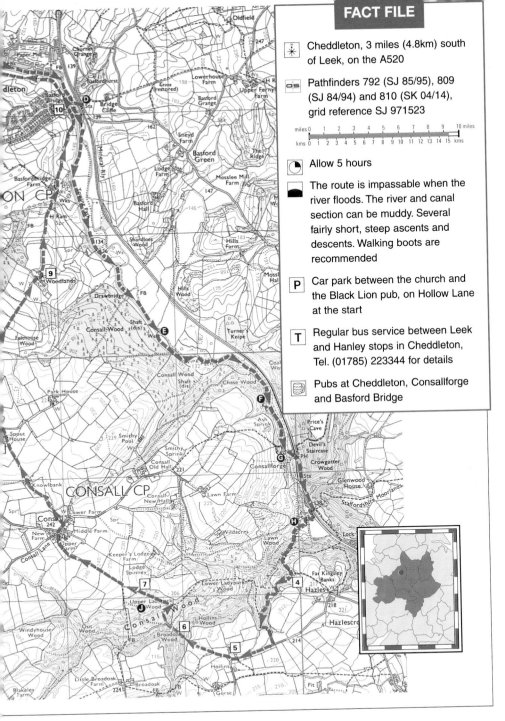

FACT FILE

✳ Cheddleton, 3 miles (4.8km) south of Leek, on the A520

▫ Pathfinders 792 (SJ 85/95), 809 (SJ 84/94) and 810 (SK 04/14), grid reference SJ 971523

miles 0 1 2 3 4 5 6 7 8 9 10 miles
kms 0 1 2 3 4 5 6 7 8 9 10 11 12 13 14 15 kms

◖ Allow 5 hours

▬ The route is impassable when the river floods. The river and canal section can be muddy. Several fairly short, steep ascents and descents. Walking boots are recommended

P Car park between the church and the Black Lion pub, on Hollow Lane at the start

T Regular bus service between Leek and Hanley stops in Cheddleton, Tel. (01785) 223344 for details

🍺 Pubs at Cheddleton, Consallforge and Basford Bridge

39

The Flint Mill

The Flint Mill, which is still powered by water, can be seen crushing flint for potteries at Stoke-on-Trent, at weekends and on some week-day afternoons.

There has been a mill at the point of the Churnet where South Mill now stands since the 13th century. Originally a corn mill, then a fulling mill, it was converted to grind flint in around 1800. Another mill, North Mill, had been built beside the same mill stream 40 years earlier for the same purpose. Both survive miraculously intact. The twin undershot wheels work machinery that is dedicated to producing raw materials for the potters in nearby Stoke-on-Trent.

Flint is an important ingredient in the manufacture of fine china and porcelain, to which it gives both strength and whiteness. It is found mainly in the chalk hills and downs of southeast England. A long journey by coaster and then by narrowboat once brought the flint to Cheddleton.

When it had been unloaded, it was roasted, then crushed, before being mixed with water and ground to fine powder in the mills. The resultant, soup-like 'slop' was allowed to settle before it was dried in a slip kiln, formed into blocks and sent on a narrow boat to the potteries.

All the work took place on this small site. The different areas are interconnected by a plateway and a series of pumps worked by the waterwheels.

Dedicated volunteers today ensure that the mills are operational. South Mill also houses machinery for the crushing of various metallic ores, which give potters a vast choice of colours for the decoration of their pots. The old miller's cottage that adjoins South Mill houses artefacts from centuries past.

The Cromford Canal

A pleasant and varied walk through 'the cradle of the industrial revolution'

Originally built to serve local industry, Cromford Canal is a haven for wildlife.

At Cromford in 1771, Richard Arkwright established his own mill with its water-powered machinery and large workforce, earning him the title 'Father of the Factory System'. Cromford Canal was built to serve the mill.

The area is rich in industrial archaeology, and the walk passes through attractive, hilly countryside which gives good views along the Derwent valley and across to the Peak District. There are many interesting sites to visit and the canal is a haven for wildlife and colourful wild flowers.

Cromford's historical Arkwright's mill **Ⓐ** is well worth a visit either at the start or finish of the walk. Part of the mill is normally open, and includes a Visitor and Exhibition Centre, shops and a café.

41

THE WALK

CROMFORD WHARF–LEA BRIDGE
The walk starts from the car park at Cromford Wharf just off the A6, 3 miles (4.8km) south of Matlock Bath.

1 From Cromford Wharf ❸ start out along the towpath, the canal on your right. Continue to High Peak Junction ❸.

2 After the junction, continue along the left bank of the canal past Lea Wood pump house ❶. Cross the aqueduct over the River Derwent. At the end of the aqueduct, cross the swing-bridge to the right-hand bank of canal. Follow path to the canal tunnel.

3 At tunnel entrance, leave the towpath by taking the ascending path on the right to the top of the small hill. Left through the kissing gate, climb path ahead through the field, keeping left of the cottage. From the cottage follow track by the high, stone wall to reach another kissing gate. Go through the gate.

4 Do not carry on along the track up to Holloway village, but turn left into the field and follow the hedgerow on your left. Cross over the drive which leads to Lea Hurst House ❸ and continue along the left-hand hedge in the next small field. Go through a gap stile in the corner, then follow the stone wall round to reach a stile by a small copse. Follow the path through the trees then, keeping to the right, go down the field, over the stile and continue down the right-hand side of the next field to the kissing gate.

5 Turn left and follow the road down into Lea Bridge. (Take care when crossing the road because of the dangerous corner.) Cross the bridge over Lea Brook, to find the footpath on the right-hand side by the gate, near the corner of the cotton spinning mills.

6 Proceed through a stone gap stile and take the footpath bearing left into Bow Wood. Follow this main path through the wood, ignoring all paths to the left and right. Continue on the track leading out of the wood to reach the lane near Castletop Farm. Proceed through the stone gap stile.

7 Turn left down the lane, which affords good views of Willersley Castle across the valley. Follow the lane down to the road.

8 Turn right, follow the road along the bank of the River Derwent, back to the car park at Cromford Wharf. Pass Willersley Castle ❸ and cross the road bridge above the river.

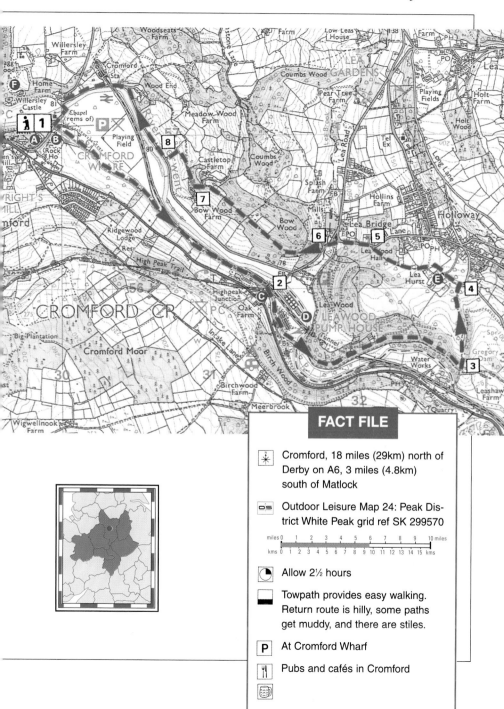

FACT FILE

☀ Cromford, 18 miles (29km) north of Derby on A6, 3 miles (4.8km) south of Matlock

OS Outdoor Leisure Map 24: Peak District White Peak grid ref SK 299570

miles 0 1 2 3 4 5 6 7 8 9 10 miles
kms 0 1 2 3 4 5 6 7 8 9 10 11 12 13 14 15 kms

◔ Allow 2½ hours

▭ Towpath provides easy walking. Return route is hilly, some paths get muddy, and there are stiles.

P At Cromford Wharf

⊗ Pubs and cafés in Cromford

Sir Richard Arkwright

Arkwright started life as a wigmaker and barber. But he went on to develop machines that revolutionized the textile industry.

Richard Arkwright was born in Preston, Lancashire, in 1732. He was the youngest of seven children, born to a tailor.

He was an inventive, enterprising man, who designed and built a machine for spinning cotton which, since it was powered by water, became known as the waterframe.

His mill at Nottingham, built in 1769, used horsepower to drive the machinery, but this was incapable of further development on a large scale. In his search for continuous water power to drive his newly invented machinery, Arkwright moved to Cromford.

He built the first mill in Cromford in 1771, and it became the world's first successful, water-powered cotton spinning mill based on a factory system. Within ten years, the mill was operating almost continuously. It employed nearly 500 workers, usually working 12-hour shifts.

At this time, Arkwright developed Cromford into one of the first industrial villages, with rows of cottages for the mill workers. The new enterprise was immensely successful, and Arkwright went on to build other mills and to license industrial machinery.

He was knighted in 1786, and appointed High Sheriff of Derbyshire in 1787. He started to build a stately home, Willersley Castle, but he died in 1793, before it was completed. He had amassed a great fortune by the time he died, leaving £500,000.

Cromford Canal was built largely as a result of Arkwright's initiative, but he did not see it completed, as it was not opened until a year after his death.

Index